THE LAW AND ECONOMICS

Your Rights as a Consumer

THE LAW AND ECONOMICS

Your Rights as a Consumer

Michael K. Walz

Series Editor: M. Barbara Killen

Lerner Publications Company ▪ Minneapolis, Minnesota

Words that appear in **bold** type are listed in a glossary that starts on page 82.

Library of Congress Cataloging-in-Publication Data

Walz, Michael K.
     The law and economics: your rights as a consumer / by Michael
K. Walz.
         p.   cm.—(Economics for today)
     Summary: Explains consumer rights, consumer protection,
warranties, credit, contracts, consumer fraud, and other areas where
the relationship between the consumer and goods and services comes
into contact with the law.
     ISBN 0-8225-1779-5
         1. Commercial law—United States—Juvenile literature.
2. Consumer protection—Law and legislation—United States—Juvenile
literature. [1. Commercial law. 2. Consumer protection—Law and
legislation.]
     I. Title. II. Series.

KF889.6.W35   1990
343.794'071—dc20
[347.940371]   89-38947
                                                       CIP
                                                        AC

Manufactured in the United States of America

1 2 3 4 5 6 7 8 9 10 99 98 97 96 95 94 93 92 91 90

CONTENTS

1 The United States Economy 6

2 The United States Legal System 10

3 Contracts 16

4 Consumer Fraud 29

5 Consumer Protection 45

6 Warranties 56

7 Damages 64

8 Credit and Collection 70

Glossary 82

Index 86

THE UNITED STATES ECONOMY

From early in the history of the human race, every society has had an economic system as a part of its organization. In primitive cultures, this usually was a **barter system** in which goods were exchanged for other goods or services. In the United States, the barter system was very much a part of pioneer life. During the late 19th century, it was not un-common for a homesteader to offer livestock or produce in exchange for medical services or the work of a blacksmith.

In the modern world, societies do not share the same ideas about

controlling the **economy**—the production, distribution, and sale of products and the regulation of money. As a result, a number of different economic systems are used throughout the world.

Some societies have an economic system known as **communism,** in which the government maintains control over the production and distribution of goods and services. For example, in a communist country, most clothing might be manufactured in government factories by government workers and sold in government stores at prices determined by the government.

Socialism is an economic system that is popular in parts of Europe and many Middle Eastern and African countries. Socialism is based on the belief that a nation's wealth should be distributed equally among all citizens and that governments should try to provide for each person's basic needs. Socialist economies vary, but in most socialist countries, there is strict government regulation of private and government-run businesses.

In contrast, the economic system in the United States is founded upon the idea of **capitalism**. In a capitalist system, citizens are free to invest their money in private businesses with the expectation of making a profit. **Laissez-faire** is a term used to describe a capitalist economy in which private businesses operate without any government interference.

Compared to businesses in communist or socialist countries, businesses in the United States are largely free from government control. This is not to say, however, that a totally laissez-faire system of capitalism operates in the United States. Rather, the federal government and the various state and local governments have enacted laws that regulate the operation of private businesses when regulation is seen to be in the best interests of all citizens.

Imagine a society in which a business is free to manufacture children's toys covered with lead-based paint that can cause brain damage or death. Think of the harm to a family that has left its automobile with a repair shop, believing the car needed repairs costing less than $100, only to learn that the shop has installed over $1,000 in new parts and will not give the car back until the family pays the entire bill. Suppose that automobile dealers were free to alter mileage indicators so that a customer could purchase a car believing it had been driven only 25,000 miles when, in fact, it had been driven three times that amount.

Reasonable rules and regulations are needed to guide our capitalist system, provide for the orderly conduct of business, and protect the rights of businesses and individuals. The laws enacted to achieve these goals are as much a part of our economic system as the idea of capitalism itself. To understand the United States economy, we must also study and understand the laws that control the economy in our ever-changing and complex society.

THE UNITED STATES LEGAL SYSTEM

To understand the United States legal system, one must first realize that it is not a single system at all. Rather, it is a tripartite, or three-part, system. The authority to make and interpret laws has been divided among three levels of government: federal, state, and local.

The federal, state, and local governments are further divided into three branches. The *legislative* branch of the federal government —the United States Congress— passes laws that affect the entire nation. The *executive* branch includes the offices of the president,

the vice president, and the secretaries of agriculture, defense, treasury, education, housing, labor, and other departments. The executive departments oversee different aspects of the national government and enforce federal laws. If disputes arise or federal laws are broken, the *judicial* branch of government—the Supreme Court and the federal courts—interprets federal laws.

State legislatures make laws that affect citizens within the geographic boundaries of each state. Governors administer the laws of the state, and state courts try cases when laws are broken or disputes arise within a state. Laws passed by state legislatures are called **statutes**.

Local governments also have legislative, executive, and judicial departments. Elected city council members and county commissioners make laws that affect city and county residents. Local government also includes other rule-making agencies, such as school boards. The laws that city officials pass are called **ordinances**. Most cities have an executive, usually called a mayor, who oversees the operations of city government. Some larger cities have municipal (city) courts that enforce and interpret city ordinances.

Regulations established by other local bodies of government, such as a school board (sometimes called a board of education), can have the effect of law and may even be enforced by the state courts. The board of education for a school district, for example, will set the calendar for the school year, specify the days school will be in session, and set the hours of the school day. A student who does not attend classes at these times without a reasonable excuse might be charged with truancy and tried in the state juvenile court.

The school board is the governing body for a school district. Rules set by a school board can be enforced by the state courts.

There are two types of law in the United States: civil and criminal. In general, **civil law** can be defined as the collection of laws that govern disputes between individuals. Often, one of the participants in a civil lawsuit seeks money from another individual or organization. Sometimes, however, the object of the lawsuit is to gain an **injunction**—a court order telling the opposing party to do or not to do a particular thing.

What if the highway department in your town announced that it was going to build a road near your home, and you knew that the roadway would cut through a marshland that is home to many birds and animals? As a citizen concerned with ecology, you might seek an injunction to prevent the building of the road until there had been a study to determine the effect that the road would have on the wildlife in the area.

Civil law covers many areas of legal practice and includes the laws regulating personal property, real property (land, buildings, and structures permanently attached to the land), banking and commerce, and family life (marriage, divorce, and adoption).

Because crime harms all members of society, the government—not the individual victim of a crime—brings charges in a criminal case.

While civil law is concerned with relationships and disputes between private individuals, **criminal law** is concerned with disputes between a **defendant** and the government. Criminal law applies to theft, traffic violations, assault, murder, and other acts that are considered destructive to society. Under the criminal law, the government is always recognized as the victim of a crime. There are two reasons why this is so. First of all, if individual victims of crime were forced to hire their own attorneys to prosecute, or try, their cases in court, the poor might not have enough money to protect their rights under the criminal law. Secondly, criminal behavior harms all members of society. It is appropriate, therefore, for the society as a whole to act as the complaining party in a criminal case and to hire the prosecuting attorney at government expense.

A person becomes **liable** under the law when he or she violates a criminal statute or fails to meet a civil obligation. Sometimes a person can be liable under both the civil and the criminal law for a single act.

Suppose Mark left a dinner party after drinking too much alcohol. He fell asleep at the wheel and his car sideswiped Colleen's van as she was driving through an intersection on a green light. Mark would be liable under the criminal law for running the light and driving while intoxicated. Colleen may also **sue** Mark under civil law for the cost of repairing her van and for any medical bills arising from the incident.

It is important to remember that not all states and cities have identical laws. For example, gambling is a crime in some states, but not in others. Because laws differ from state to state and city to city, no book can possibly provide information on all of the laws that exist on a given subject. Also, certain laws, like the federal income tax code, are extremely complex. This book, therefore, deals only with general concepts of law that affect the economic affairs of average citizens.

The Minnesota State Capitol. Here, state legislators make laws, or statutes. Statutes differ from state to state.

CONTRACTS

A **contract** is an agreement between two or more "parties" that can be enforced in court. In the simplest contracts, the parties are individuals. In more complicated agreements, the parties may be large corporations or governments.

Many of our ideas about contracts arose in England during the Middle Ages (A.D. 500 to about A.D. 1500). Most of us think of the Middle Ages as a time of kings and castles. It also was the period of history that marked the development of England's **Common Law,** which

is the foundation of nearly all of the legal systems in the United States. Only Louisiana, which traces its legal history to the French **Code of Napoleon**, does not share this Common Law heritage.

Under the Common Law, there were seven requirements for a legal contract. These requirements still apply to contracts made in the United States.

Offer

No contract can be formed without an offer. An offer is made when one party indicates a willingness to enter into a bargain. This may be a bargain to sell or buy some object or, perhaps, to perform a service.

If Crazy Cal's Classic Cars placed an ad in a newspaper stating that it would sell a 1960 Ford Thunderbird for $4,000, this would be a legal offer. If a student placed a newspaper ad offering to do yard work for $4 an hour, this would also be a legal offer.

Acceptance

Once an offer is made by one party to a contract, the other party must give his or her acceptance of the offer. In many cases, this is done by signing a formal written contract. If Michael goes to Crazy Cal's lot and signs an agreement promising to pay $4,000 for the advertised Thunderbird, he has accepted Cal's offer.

In other cases, a party may accept an offer verbally. Suppose Patricia owns an Italian restaurant. She phones her supplier and orders several hundred cans of tomato sauce. The supplier agrees, and makes the delivery the

A store owner has placed an order by phone, and a warehouse worker prepares the shipment. The customer must pay for the goods, even though no written contract has been made.

following morning. Patricia must pay for the tomato sauce even though she has not signed a contract.

Sometimes, acceptance can be given and a contract formed without a written or spoken agreement. Suppose Kacy raises her hand at an auction sale to bid on a bicycle. There are no higher bidders. The auctioneer is obligated to sell the bicycle to Kacy at the price she has bid, and she is obligated to buy it at that price, although no written contract exists and no words of acceptance have been spoken.

Consideration

In every contract, both parties must offer some form of **consideration** (something of value) to the other party. Crazy Cal, for example, has offered to sell a Thunderbird for $4,000 and Michael has accepted the offer at that price. The car's value is Cal's consideration. Michael's consideration is his money.

At an auction, customers often make bids by raising their hands. When the highest bid is made, a contract is formed—even though there is no written or spoken agreement.

Performance of Prior Conditions

Sometimes one of the parties to a contract must perform some act before the contract becomes legally binding. If that act is not done, then no contract has been created. For example, Jeanne offered to pay a painter $3,000 to paint her home. The painter is only entitled to the money if he finishes painting Jeanne's house. If he does not do the work, there is no contract and Jeanne is not obligated to pay.

Competent Parties

Both parties to a contract must be competent, that is, legally capable of entering into a binding agreement. Sometimes a party to a contract is found to be incompetent because of a serious mental disability. The most common reason for a person to be considered incompetent to enter into a contract, however, is because he or she is too young.

The **age of majority** is the age at which a person becomes an adult and is considered able to take charge of his or her own legal affairs. While the age of majority varies, in most states it is 18. Before people reach the age of legal independence, they are said to be **minors**.

Depending on the circumstances, contracts between adults and minors may be valid, void, or voidable. A **valid** contract is legal in all cases and can be enforced in a court of law. In some cases, a minor can enter into a valid contract. For example, a valid contract exists when a minor purchases necessities such as food, shelter, or clothing. Since all people need these things to live, a minor can be held to a promise to pay for them.

Consumers eat lunch at a fast-food restaurant. They haven't signed contracts, but they are legally obligated to pay for their meals.

Suppose Ryan, age 15, enters a restaurant and orders a hamburger and a soft drink. The food is cooked and delivered to Ryan's table. Although Ryan is a minor, he is legally obligated to pay for his meal.

However, contracts with minors are **void** if the law of the state where the contract has been made requires that person to reach the age of majority before entering into a legal agreement.

The law in Christopher's state specifies that people under the age of 18 cannot buy automobiles on an installment payment plan. Suppose Christopher purchases a car from Crazy Cal and promises to pay $100 per month until the full price is paid. Christopher does not make the payments. Although Crazy Cal is entitled to the return of the car, he cannot take Christopher to court for the rest of the payments, because their contract was illegal. The contract between Christopher and Crazy Cal is considered void.

A **voidable** contract is one that is valid unless it is voided, or cancelled, by one of the parties. Most contracts made between an adult and a minor may be made valid or voided by the minor, but not by the adult.

Suppose that the Burger Barn was going out of business. Kelly, age 16, had long admired the old jukebox in the establishment and offered to buy it for $100. The owner quickly agreed and Kelly went home to get the money. Before Kelly returned, a collector saw the jukebox and offered to buy it for $1,000. The owner of the Burger Barn attempted to cancel the agreement with Kelly, claiming that because Kelly was a minor, no valid contract had been created. In most states, the owner would have to sell the jukebox to Kelly. A contract with a minor is voidable at the option of the minor. It cannot be cancelled by the adult party.

A minor may choose to void a contract at any time. But once he or she reaches the age of majority, the contract will become binding if it is not cancelled within a reasonable time.

Shelly was 17 when she signed a written contract promising to pay a health club $50 a month for three years to become a lifetime member. One week after turning 18, Shelly sent a notice to the health club cancelling the contract. In most states, the club would be required to release Shelly from the agreement. She was a minor when the contract was formed, membership in a health club is not a human necessity, and Shelly gave her notice of cancellation within a reasonable time after reaching the age of majority. She must, however, pay for the months she actually used the club before the contract was cancelled. If Shelly continued to use the club for several months after turning 18, she could be said to have ratified, or approved, the contract, and she would be obligated to pay for the entire 36-month period.

Legal Purpose

A contract is void if it does not have a legal purpose. That is, the courts will not enforce an agreement to do something that is unlawful.

Chuck lives in a state that prohibits the manufacture or sale of any gambling devices. Chuck was badly in need of money to operate his print shop. When a customer asked him to print several thousand pull tabs, he agreed to do so, even though he knew pull tabs were gambling cards. He printed the pull tabs and delivered them to the customer, who promised to pay in full at the end of the week. The customer did not pay, but Chuck cannot sue the customer for the amount due, because the contract was made for an illegal purpose.

Proper Form

Under the Common Law, certain contracts were required to be made in writing. These included contracts for the sale of land, contracts for a service that would not be fully performed within one year, and contracts for the sale of goods for more than a specific price.

Sometimes, one party must perform a particular act before a contract is legally binding. If you hire a workman to repair your sidewalk, you only have to pay if the workman finishes the job.

Some contracts must be in writing. Contracts for the sale of land, cars, and houses, for instance, are usually written agreements.

The legal requirement that certain contracts must be in writing has been carried into modern times. In all states, contracts transferring land from one party to another must be made in writing and must be filed with the county or state government where the land is located. Many states also require other kinds of contracts to be in writing. These might include contracts for the sale of new automobiles and loan agreements.

Larry agreed to buy 40 acres of lakeshore property from Lowe for $1,000 an acre. They shook hands on the agreement and Larry paid Lowe $4,000, promising to get a loan and pay the rest of the money within 30 days. Two days later, Lowe sold the same land to Proctor Properties for $1,500 an acre. Proctor paid cash for the land and received a signed deed, or contract, from Lowe. The deed was filed with the county in compliance with a state law that required all land sales to be made in writing and recorded with the county government. Although Larry was first to purchase the land, he failed to put the transaction in writing and properly record it with the county. Proctor, not Larry, will get the land, and Larry is entitled to the return of his $4,000.

Contracts are used in the business world to create agreements that can be enforced in a court of law. Because a legal obligation is created whenever a contract is made, it is important that all individuals understand their legal rights.

4

POLICE
INVESTIGATIVE
108 HOMICIDE
108 ROBBERY
110 NARCOTICS & VICE
FORGERY / FRAUD
116 PROPERTY CRIME
BURGLARY, THEFT,
126 INTERNAL AFFAIRS
130 JUVENILE

CONSUMER FRAUD

You have probably heard the expression "forewarned is forearmed." This means that if you know that an unpleasant situation might occur, you can take steps to prepare for it.

Consumers, or buyers, in the United States economy must become forewarned to a number of pitfalls that can harm their financial well-being if they are not prepared. These pitfalls often take the form of schemes to defraud consumers. When we say that something is a fraud, we mean that it is not really what it appears to be. The term "defraud" describes a situation in which someone intentionally misrepresents an important part of a contract to the other party. For example, telling a buyer that a product is "brand-new" when, in fact, it is used would be a way of defrauding that buyer.

There are many forms of consumer fraud. Regardless of the form, all consumer fraud involves lying, cheating, and stealing.

Bait-and-Switch

In the classic bait-and-switch maneuver, a retail business advertises a product at an extremely low price, but has no intention of selling the product at that price. The "bait," of course, is the promise of an extraordinary bargain. When the customer comes to the store in search of the item, the bait-and-switch operator will try to "switch" the customer's attention to a higher-priced model, claiming that the advertised product has undesirable features. If the customer continues to ask for the advertised model at the sale price, the retailer will often claim that the item has been sold out.

There are two forms of bait-and-switch: the "highball" and the "lowball." The highball sometimes happens at automobile dealerships when a consumer trades in a used car, and the value of the old car is deducted from the purchase price of a new vehicle. In the highball scheme, the salesperson might offer a trade-in price that is more generous than the company can really afford to give. The salesperson intends to make up the difference by switching the customer to a higher-priced car or persuading the customer to buy expensive options.

One automobile dealer advertised that he would give customers the highest trade-in price that was available anywhere. Attracted to the car lot by the ad, Sean was quoted a trade-in price for his old car that was several hundred dollars higher than the figures given by any other dealer he had visited. After agreeing to buy a new car on the terms quoted, Sean was then told that the car he wanted had just been sold, but a higher-priced model was still available.

Sometimes advertisers lure customers with sales and specials. In the store, however, the customer might be switched from the advertised special to a higher-priced item.

Most businesses are honest and want to give the customer a good deal.

By being manipulated into buying a more expensive car, Sean lost the benefit of the high trade-in price. The dealer, in turn, made up for the generous trade-in allowance by making a greater profit on the sale of the higher-priced car.

A lowball bait-and-switch occurs when a salesperson quotes a lower price for an item than the company can possibly afford. The object of this scheme is to attract the customer by appearing to undersell the competition. As with the highball, the dealer's true intention is to make up for the low price by switching the customer to a more expensive model or convincing the customer to purchase expensive options for the advertised model.

An electronics dealer, for example, might offer to sell

a name-brand giant-screen color television set at a price much lower than that advertised by the competition. Customers arriving at the store to purchase the advertised set might be told that the picture clarity of the set was rated "poor" by a leading consumer magazine, but a more expensive television was rated "near the top." If the customers still wanted to buy the advertised set, the salespeople might claim that the television would not work properly without an optional installation kit, available only at substantial additional cost.

The reason for using bait-and-switch advertising is, of course, to attract customers into the advertiser's store. The bait-and-switch operator hopes that although some people may leave the store after learning that the advertised bargain is not available, many others will remain and buy a higher-priced model or decide to buy expensive options. In short, the bait-and-switch is a scheme to attract customers fraudulently—and for this reason, it is illegal.

Phony Going-out-of-Business Sales

In this type of consumer fraud, a company announces that it is going out of business and must sell its remaining merchandise. It then stocks up on additional merchandise—often of inferior quality to the products that it normally sells—to prolong the sale and increase profits. In extreme cases, stores have had phony going-out-of-business sales that lasted for over a year!

Some states have attempted to curb this type of fraud by passing laws that prohibit going-out-of-business sales from lasting more than a specified number of days.

A bicycle mechanic trues a wheel. Before he begins his work, the mechanic will give the customer an estimate of how much the job will cost.

Service and Repair Schemes

A **mechanic's lien** gives mechanics and others who repair consumer goods the right to keep an item until the customer pays in full for repairs. In many states, a mechanic's lien is automatically created at the time the repairs are made. It is not necessary for the repair shop to go to court or hire a lawyer to obtain the lien.

Imagine for a moment that your expensive bicycle needs adjustment. The repairman you have selected has quoted you a price of $50 for the repairs. Two days later, you are notified that the repairs have been completed and you can pick up your bike. When you arrive at the shop, the repairman presents you with a bill for $150, claiming that after he took the bike apart he found several broken parts that were not visible during his first inspection. Using the bike without replacing the parts would be dangerous, the mechanic states, so he went ahead and made the repairs and supplied the additional parts that increased your bill. When you object, the repairman tells you that he has a mechanic's lien on the bike and will keep it until you make full payment.

The practice described above was common in the repair business until recently. Actually a form of bait-and-switch, the service and repair scheme uses a lowball estimate to persuade the customer to leave the item for repairs. The shop really has no intention of making the repairs at the price quoted. After the item is disassembled, other defects are "discovered" and repaired, increasing the bill far beyond the original estimate.

Many states have passed legislation that prevents repair shops from exceeding a price estimate by more than a specified amount. Minnesota, for instance, has a law that prohibits repair shops from charging more than 10 percent over the estimated cost of a repair. Therefore, a repair job estimated to cost $100 cannot exceed $110. The 10 percent increase is allowed because it is not always possible for a repair shop to determine the cost of the proposed repair with absolute certainty.

In states that do not have such protection for consumers, it is often very difficult to prove fraud on the part of the repairperson. Usually, complaints must arise from several customers about a particular business before authorities can determine that the business has engaged in a calculated scheme to defraud the consumer.

Packaging Fraud

Fraud in packaging most often occurs in businesses where it is possible to "short-weight" a customer by placing misleading labels on packages or tampering with a scale used to weigh consumer goods such as produce or meat. Gas stations have been known to defraud consumers by modifying gas pumps so that they provide a false reading on the meters.

How can you be sure that the pump is giving an accurate measurement of your gas purchase? State agencies monitor gas stations and other businesses that use weights and measures.

Some grocery items "settle" during shipment and storage. If a box of cereal is partly empty when you get it home, you are not the victim of consumer fraud.

State agencies in charge of monitoring weights and measures used in businesses have largely eliminated short-weighting. By annually inspecting butcher shops, gas stations, and other establishments that use meters and scales, state officials can ensure that the consumer is provided with accurate and honest measurements.

Some types of misrepresentation in packaging are not illegal. A breakfast cereal manufacturer will be quick to point out that some amount of "settling" is to be expected during shipment, leaving the upper part of each cereal box empty when it is opened. Because this cannot be avoided, cereal boxes usually carry a label clearly indicating that the cereal is sold by weight and not volume.

Land Schemes

From time to time, you may see newspaper and television advertisements for the sale of property in other states. Usually these ads are placed in newspapers in northern cities and offer property for sale in a southern state. The southern locations might be attractive to retired persons who wish to relocate to a warmer climate.

Often prospective buyers are encouraged to buy land without actually seeing it. They may be shown photographs or videotapes that the sellers claim accurately represent the property. The customers are usually bombarded with expressive sales language that speaks of "the retirement opportunity of a lifetime," or "your last chance to have an affordable place in the sun."

After making sizeable **down payments**, buyers might find that their place in the sun has no water or is under water. The land may be surrounded by property owned by other people, with no means for the owner to get in or out without trespassing. Possibly the property is far from any source of electricity or other utilities. In short, the land may be nearly worthless.

Of course, not all companies selling land are out to defraud their customers. But consumers should be on guard, particularly if the seller attempts to force a quick decision or offers bonuses if the contract is signed right away. The best course of action is for the consumer to examine the property before entering into an agreement.

Advance-Fee Schemes

When a consumer is persuaded to pay in advance for services the salesperson has no intention of providing, the customer is a victim of an advance-fee scheme. Usually, the advance-fee operator runs an advertisement that offers a product or service at an extraordinarily low price. The operator might set up business at a motel and use the room phone to answer calls from customers. He or she then persuades customers to buy the product or service, telling them that the offer is "for a limited time only." Usually, a substantial down payment is requested. After collecting the down payment, the advance-fee operator leaves town without delivering the product or performing the service.

For instance, an advance-fee operator, aware that a growing number of homeowners hire lawn services to apply weed killer and fertilizer to their lawns during the summer, might place this ad in a local paper:

QUALITY LAWN CARE AT LOW, LOW COST! WE GUARANTEE WE WILL BEAT OUR COMPETITION BY AT LEAST TWENTY PERCENT! YOUR MONEY REFUNDED IF NOT FULLY SATISFIED! FOR A HEALTHY LAWN AND A HEALTHY POCKETBOOK, CALL 348-3115 TODAY!

People who respond to the ad are given appointments to have their lawns inspected. The operator measures the homeowners' yards and examines the condition of their grass. The operator then quotes a price far below that of any other lawn service. Homeowners are told that they have to make a down payment of 50 percent of the total price to begin service and that they can receive a 10 percent discount by paying the entire cost in advance.

After waiting many days for the promised service to begin, the customers then learn that the operator, like their money, is gone.

Beware of ads that seem too good to be true. Many land scheme and advance-fee operators advertise in local papers. After making a sizeable down payment, the customer often finds that the advertised land is worthless or the advance-fee operator has left town.

Charity Fraud

Most charitable organizations in the United States are run by honest individuals with a sincere desire to work on a social problem or to advance a social goal. Some charities serve the needs of the poor, while others assist the handicapped. Some promote drama, art, or music, while others pay for missionary work or establish inner-city youth programs. Thousands of legitimate charities provide a wide range of services to the public.

However, organizations that disguise themselves as charities to gain illegal profit are exposed from time to time. Some of these groups, claiming to have a charitable purpose, ask for contributions, but have no intention of using the money for anything other than to pad the pockets of the organizers. Others may send salespeople door-to-door to sell candy or other small items and claim that the profits will go to charity. Again, the money will only benefit the operators of the illegal scheme.

The office of the attorney general in most states has a list of charities that have registered to operate within that state. If you have a question as to whether a charity is legitimate, it is wise to check the credentials of the organization before making a contribution.

Chain Referral Schemes

The products sold by operators of chain referral schemes are often overpriced or of low quality. The buyer is told that he or she will be able to recover the cost of the product by referring the salesperson to more potential customers. The buyer is supposed to receive a commission, or portion of the purchase price, for every referral that results in a sale. Often, however, the buyer is not able to refer enough new customers to cover the cost of the product, and he or she is left to pay a high price for goods of inferior quality.

Imagine that a door-to-door salesman told a homeowner that she could receive an entire set of encyclopedias for free, simply by providing the salesman with the names of prospective customers. The homeowner was told she would receive a commission of $50 for every sale actually made to one of these referrals. The customer signed a contract that stated that the price for the set of books was $1,000. The contract also stated that she would receive a commission of $50 for each referral resulting in a sale, and that the commission would be deducted from the price of the books. The homeowner gave the salesman a list of 20 prospective customers, but only one person on the list actually bought a set of encyclopedias. The homeowner was then obligated to pay the company $950.

Business-Opportunity Schemes

The business-opportunity scheme is designed to lure people into investing in a worthless business. In this operation, an advertisement promises a high income for manufacturing some product or performing some service, often in your own home. The work can range from addressing and stuffing envelopes to making a small product.

The advertiser might tell people that they can make a considerable sum of money, perhaps as much as $1,000 per month, in their spare time by preparing special mailings for small businesses. The promoter will then offer to sell the individual a list of businesses that might use this type of service. The person soon learns, however, that most modern businesses use computers to prepare their mailings. The few businesses that might be interested in a home-based service are highly sought after by others who are also trying to start a work-at-home business. Finally, the individual who is fortunate enough to find work will learn that businesses are willing to pay only a small sum, perhaps a few cents per envelope, to have their mailings prepared.

Sometimes the objective of the work-at-home operator is simply to persuade the victim to invest in expensive equipment. Christy, for example, answered an ad that promised she could earn up to $25,000 a year manufacturing plastic novelty buttons in her own home. Christy paid the advertiser $700 for the machine needed to make the buttons, and also ordered $300 worth of plastic, pins, and other materials. She was told that the advertiser was a nationally known wholesaler of novelty items and would likely be placing many orders with her. Christy made 1,000 buttons but received no orders. Of course, the company had never really promised to buy anything from Christy; it had merely said it "likely" would be placing orders. Christy was left with an expensive machine, the remainder of her materials, and 1,000 novelty buttons she could not sell.

Because there are so many types of consumer fraud, it is impossible to protect all of the consumers all of the time. The best protection is to be suspicious of bargains that seem "too good to be true" and to become familiar with the consumer protection laws that are explained in the next chapter.

5

CONSUMER PROTECTION

The Latin phrase *caveat emptor* means "let the buyer beware." Historically, the phrase meant that the buyer of consumer goods should assume the risk that the goods might not work properly. In ancient times, if a farmer bought a cow that could not produce milk, the doctrine of caveat emptor prevented the farmer from returning the cow to the seller.

In our legal system, the doctrine of caveat emptor still applies to the sale of a few types of consumer goods. For example, it is a general rule that no guarantee exists on a used item. In fact, if you attend an auction sale, you will likely be told that each item is being sold "as is" and "with all faults." This is the auctioneer's way of saying that because the goods are used, the buyer must assume the risk that they will not work properly.

However, many states have passed consumer protection laws that replace the doctrine of caveat emptor. These laws give consumers special rights when purchasing new items, services, and some used products.

Door-to-Door Sales

Many states have passed laws to regulate door-to-door sales. These states recognize that most salespeople who work door-to-door receive little or no salary. Rather, the salespeople make their money through a commission— a percentage of the purchase price of each sale they make. To be successful, door-to-door salespeople must learn what motivates consumers and use that knowledge to persuade people to make purchases. Door-to-door salespeople are often expert communicators. Customers may buy products they really do not want or need because they have fallen victim to the skillful persuasion of an accomplished door-to-door salesperson.

One day an encyclopedia salesperson knocked on Mr. Conway's door and announced that her company had done a study of the neighborhood. Mr. Conway was told that the study revealed him to be a trendsetter on the block. All of his neighbors, the saleswoman said, looked up to him and wanted to follow his example. Mr. Conway was flattered that his neighbors thought so highly of him. He didn't think it strange, then, when the saleswoman said that he could get a free set of encyclopedias simply by allowing the company to put a set in his home. The woman convinced Mr. Conway that once his neighbors saw the books in his home, they would want to be like him and have their own encyclopedias. The saleswoman promised to give Mr. Conway a commission from each sale she made to his friends and neighbors. He was told that these commissions could be used to pay for the set of books in his home.

We have seen that this is a chain-referral form of consumer fraud. You may wonder why anyone would fall victim to such an obvious form of marketing manipulation, but many people do.

Because door-to-door salespeople can persuade consumers to buy expensive products they may not need or cannot afford, the law in many states provides for a "cooling-off period" of several days before a door-to-door sales contract is final. A typical law may require a three-day waiting period following a door-to-door sale. During this time, the customer may cancel the agreement without having to provide any reason for doing so. Upon receipt of the cancellation notice, the salesperson must promptly return any down payment the customer has made. In some states, the customer may keep the product until the salesperson returns the down payment.

Club Contracts

Consumer protection spokespeople have found that many of the persuasive techniques used in door-to-door

Many states give consumers a brief "cooling-off period" during which they may cancel a contract for a health or dating club.

sales are also used to convince people to join certain types of clubs. People who join health clubs and dating clubs, for instance, may find that their state applies a "cooling-off period" to the contracts they sign when they become members.

Anne, age 18, wanted to lose weight before starting college. She decided to accept the invitation of a local health club to use their facilities during a free visit. After trying out the exercise equipment and pool and attending an aerobics class, Anne was asked to meet with a fitness counselor.

Anne felt somewhat intimidated by the thin, attractive woman who checked her height and weight. Anne was then asked if she smoked cigarettes, and, somewhat ashamedly, she replied that she did. The counselor said that for less than the price of one package of cigarettes a day, Anne could belong to the club. She suggested that, by giving up smoking, Anne would be joining the club for free because she would not be spending any money she was not spending already.

Of course, the club did not want Anne to drop by and pay a few dollars each day. The counselor had her sign a contract requiring her to pay a total of $1,000 over a period of three years. Anne signed.

Upon returning home, Anne began to realize that joining the club would hurt her ability to help pay for her college tuition. She quickly came to regret her decision to sign the contract.

Anne checked with the attorney general's office and learned that the law in her state provides for a three-day cooling-off period after health club contracts are signed. Anne sent the club a written notice of cancellation within the three-day period. She was no longer obligated by the contract.

Most health and athletic clubs are totally honest businesses. Many clubs permit members to belong on a month-to-month basis after an initial membership fee is paid. This allows members to quit at the end of any month they choose. However, some clubs, such as the one Anne selected, ask customers to become "lifetime members" or require long-term membership contracts. These commitments may not be in the best interests of the customer.

If a mechanic finds that your car needs more repairs than were originally authorized, the shop must ask your permission to perform the extra work.

Estimates for Repairs

We have learned that a mechanic's lien may be created when someone takes an item in for repairs. The lien allows the shop to keep the item until the repair bill has been paid. We have also learned that some unscrupulous repair shops use a service and repair scheme to inflate their bills and force consumers to pay for unneeded repairs and parts. To correct these abuses, the laws in many states say that if a consumer requests a written estimate of the cost of repairs, the shop must provide it.

Sometimes it is necessary for a repair shop to take apart an item to determine why it will not work properly. In such cases, the shop is allowed to charge an appropriate fee for the work involved in performing the inspection. However, the law usually says that the shop cannot charge for providing the written estimate unless the consumer has been notified in advance that there will be a fee. Once an estimate has been made, the shop may not charge more than the estimated amount unless the customer authorizes the additional repairs.

One day Paulette left her car with a repair shop for a tune-up and wheel alignment. She received a written estimate of $75 for the work. While aligning the wheels, the mechanic found that a part of the mechanism that joins the wheel to the steering assembly had cracked and needed to be replaced. The mechanic phoned Paulette and explained the problem, stating that the new part would cost $80 and there would be a $20 installation fee. Paulette authorized the work and became obligated to pay for the additional cost.

Some states permit a repair shop to exceed the estimate by a small amount, usually not more than 10 percent, without contacting the consumer. For example, a mechanic might take apart an engine and find that a gasket or bolt needs replacing. The mechanic need not contact the consumer to get approval for such a minor addition to the estimate.

However, when Tom took his car in for repairs, he was provided with a written estimate of $400 for the work. Tom's state allows for excess costs of not more than 10 percent of the estimated cost of the repair, unless there has been customer authorization. When he picked up the car, Tom was told that additional repairs were needed. He received a bill for $500. Because Tom did not authorize the additional repairs, he is only obligated to pay $440 (the estimated cost plus 10 percent).

Unsolicited Goods

Sometimes charitable organizations asking for contributions mail potential donors a small gift along with a request for a donation. These gifts are usually inexpensive objects such as keychains or address labels. Obviously, the organizations that send the gifts hope that the recipients will make a donation. Some people may feel obligated to pay for the item they have received, even though they didn't order it.

The general rule throughout the United States is that if you receive an item that you did not order, you may keep the item without having to pay the sender. The law regards the item as a gift.

Electronic Price Scanning

You have probably noticed the striped "bar code" labels on many consumer items. These labels are often found on merchandise in large grocery and department stores. The bar code imprints allow a laser beam to "read" the correct price of an item and record the purchase on a computer. This system allows cashiers to ring up sales quickly and provides the store with an accurate record of its sales and stock.

Some states have enacted laws that require store owners to use written prices in addition to bar codes, so that consumers can determine the cost of an item at a glance. These prices must either be on the package itself or clearly displayed on the shelf near the product. A few states also require that if the price is only displayed on the shelf, the store must provide the customer with a pen to write the price on the package. These protections allow the customer to compare the prices of different brands when making a selection, and keep store owners from surprising customers at the checkout counter with high prices.

When you rent an apartment, you will probably pay a "security deposit." If you leave the apartment in good condition, you are entitled to the return of your security deposit, plus interest.

Security Deposits

When a person rents an apartment or signs up for gas or electricity service, the landlord and the utility companies may require payment of a **security deposit.** This money is kept as security, or payment, for any future damage to the property or failure to pay utility bills.

Most states require landlords and utility companies to return the security deposit within a short period of time after the renter moves from the dwelling. The landlord may keep the deposit only if he or she tells the renter why the money is being withheld. If the landlord doesn't give a reason within the time allowed by law, the deposit must be returned to the renter.

If the landlord keeps the security deposit, he or she usually will use it to repair any damage that the renter has done to the property. It is improper for the landlord to keep the deposit simply to pay for ordinary upkeep (routine cleaning and painting).

In most states, a landlord must also pay the renter **interest** on the security deposit. Interest is a fee that is paid for the use of another person's money. Since landlords and utility companies are able to use a renter's deposit money during the entire time he or she lives in an apartment, it is only fair that they should pay interest to the renter.

Suppose that the law in Susan's state says that landlords must pay interest at the rate of 6 percent per year on all security deposits. Susan made a security deposit of $100 upon moving into her apartment and lived there for one year. If she left the apartment in good condition, she is entitled to receive $106—her $100 deposit plus 6 percent interest.

Similarly, if a gas or electric company requires that a customer make a security deposit before starting service, most states require an interest payment on the deposit. Usually the company pays the interest by deducting it from the customer's bill.

Suppose Susan paid a $50 security deposit when she

began electric service at her apartment. The law in Susan's state requires interest payments at the rate of 6 percent per year on all security deposits. Susan's final bill for electric service was $60. But because Susan was entitled to her security deposit plus interest, the company's final bill showed that Susan owed only $7—$60 minus a security deposit of $50 and an interest payment of $3.

Most businesses are not out to defraud their customers. But when dealing with large companies, consumers are often at a disadvantage. By understanding consumer protection laws and regulations, individuals can make better economic decisions and can better protect their rights in the case of a dispute.

WARRANTIES

Consumer protection law has diminished the rule of caveat emptor in modern times. Another device that protects consumers in the marketplace is the **warranty**. A warranty is a guarantee made by the manufacturer or seller of a product to the buyer. There are several different kinds of warranties.

Express Warranty

An express warranty is a guarantee that can be either spoken or in writing. A typical express

warranty that accompanies a new motorcycle might read: "The manufacturer warrants this motorcycle to be free of defects in parts and workmanship for 12 months from the date of sale, or 12,000 miles, whichever is first to occur."

To create an express warranty, it is not necessary that the words "guarantee" or "warrant" are actually used. In the case of *McCormick v. Hankscraft,* the Hankscraft Vaporizer Company manufactured a vaporizer that came with an instruction booklet explaining how the product should be used. The booklet stated that the vaporizer was "safe, tip-proof, and practically foolproof." The booklet did not mention that water in the vaporizer became scalding hot when the device was in operation. The cover of the booklet showed a young child sleeping in bed, with the vaporizer close by. A consumer named McCormick bought the vaporizer for his child's bedroom. McCormick's child woke during the night, tipped the unit over, and was severely burned by scalding water.

In this case, the court held that the photograph on the booklet cover, together with the words "safe, tip-proof, and practically foolproof" created an express warranty that the unit could be safely placed and operated near a child's bedside. The Hankscraft Company was found responsible for the injury to the child.

Limited Warranty

If an express warranty is effective for only a certain period of time or under specified conditions it is called a **limited warranty**.

When you are shopping for your first new car, you might ask the salesperson what warranty coverage is available. The salesperson might tell you that the car is guaranteed for five years or 50,000 miles. The actual warranty might read as follows:

"The manufacturer and seller warrant the engine and transmission of this vehicle to be free of defects in parts and workmanship for a period of five years from the date of sale or for 50,000 miles, whichever is first to occur. If a defect is proven to exist during the warranty period, the defective part will be repaired or replaced at the option of the manufacturer or seller without cost to the original owner."

In this example, the manufacturer and seller have limited their liability in a number of ways. First of all, only the engine and transmission are covered by the warranty. Problems with the electrical system, for

Many new cars come with a warranty. A limited warranty, however, won't cover everything that might go wrong.

example, are not included. Second, liability does not extend beyond five years or 50,000 miles, whichever comes first. In addition, the solution to any problems that might occur with the automobile is limited to repair or replacement of defective parts. The manufacturer and seller are not promising to pay compensation for injuries that might arise because of the defective parts. What is more, only the manufacturer and seller may determine whether to repair or replace a part. The car owner has no part in the decision. Finally, the warranty only protects the original owner of the car. If the car is sold after one year and 12,000 miles, the manufacturer and seller need not honor the warranty. It is not transferable to the new owner.

Implied Warranty

An **implied warranty** is a guarantee that is neither spoken nor in writing. Rather, it is created because a consumer has a right to expect that a new product will perform safely and properly. There are several different types of implied warranties.

An "implied warranty of merchantability" applies to newly purchased consumer goods. This warranty exists because the customer has the right to expect that the product he or she has just purchased will be safe to use.

In the case of *Henningson v. Bloomfield Motors,* Mr. Henningson bought a Chrysler automobile from Bloomfield Motors. The car's steering mechanism was defective, and Mrs. Henningson was seriously injured while she was driving the car. When Mr. Henningson bought the car, he signed a contract which said, in fine

No warranty exists on the sale of used goods. If you buy a secondhand item at an auction or a garage sale, you assume the risk that the item may be defective.

print on the reverse side, that Chrysler and the dealer gave no warranties other than that they would replace defective parts for 90 days from the date of sale. Chrysler and Bloomfield Motors argued that they were responsible for the repair of the car's steering mechanism, but they would not pay Mrs. Henningson's medical bills.

The court ruled that, in addition to the limited warranty contained in the contract, an implied warranty of merchantability is created whenever a new car is sold. The consumer has the right to believe that a new car will be safe to drive. This implied warranty of merchantability applies not only to the buyer, but also to other people who drive or ride in the car.

An implied warranty of merchantability does not apply to the sale of used cars, however. No warranty of any kind is created upon the sale of a used item unless there is an express warranty. If the seller wishes to do so, he or she may give a guarantee to the buyer, but without a written or spoken guarantee, no warranty exists.

In *Pokrajac v. Wade Motors,* Pokrajac bought a used car from Wade Motors and signed a contract agreeing to take the vehicle "as is" and "with no guarantees." Pokrajac found the brakes to be faulty and asked Wade to work on them. Wade did so, but Pokrajac still felt the brakes were not functioning properly. He returned to Wade Motors a second time, but Wade refused to perform any more repairs for free. The brakes failed and Pokrajac was injured. The court ruled that a person who buys secondhand items without a guarantee must assume the risk that the item may be defective. Wade was not held accountable for Pokrajac's injuries.

An "implied warranty of fitness" is created when a consumer tells a salesperson that an item is needed to handle a specific job, and the salesperson recommends a certain product. If the salesperson says that the particular product will do the job, he or she is giving a guarantee.

If a salesperson recommends a specific product for a specific job, an "implied warranty of fitness" has been created.

Suppose Wally enters the hardware store and tells the clerk he wants to mount a telephone antenna on the roof of his car and needs a drill bit that can drill through metal. If the clerk shows Wally a bit and says, "This will do the job for you," and Wally buys the bit, an implied warranty of fitness has been created. The clerk has guaranteed that the bit will safely drill through metal and do the work Wally requires.

An "implied warranty of wholesomeness" exists on food products because the consumer has the right to believe that food sold for human consumption is pure and safe to eat.

In the case of *Cushing v. Rodman,* Cushing purchased a breakfast roll at a drugstore lunch counter. The drugstore had purchased the roll from a bakery. The roll contained a pebble, which broke Cushing's tooth. The court said that even though the drugstore had no way of knowing that the pebble was in the roll, the drugstore was responsible for the damage. An implied warranty of wholesomeness was created when the drugstore sold the roll.

Often, food products reach the consumer in sealed containers. In such cases, the manufacturer is said to have created an implied warranty of wholesomeness and will be held liable if the food is not pure.

In *LeBlanc v. Coca-Cola,* LeBlanc became ill after drinking a bottle of Coca-Cola that contained a dead housefly. The court ruled that when a food product leaves the manufacturer in a sealed container, an implied warranty of wholesomeness is created. Although no one saw the fly enter the bottle at the Coca-Cola plant, it is reasonable to assume that it did so.

DAMAGES

In the case of *LeBlanc v. Coca-Cola,* the court awarded **damages** to LeBlanc as compensation for his illness. If you are legally responsible for injury to another person or damage to another's property, you are said to be *liable* for that injury or damage. If an individual or company is found to be liable, it is usually expected to pay damages—in the form of money —to the injured person. There are several different kinds of damages.

Compensatory damages are meant to pay the injured party

for the actual expenses connected with injury or property loss. Such things as medical expenses or the cost to replace damaged property are included in compensatory damages.

Future damages are a form of compensatory damages that are awarded for costs that are certain to arise at a later time following injury or property loss. For example, a person injured in an automobile accident may require a lifetime of medical care. Perhaps the injury will keep the victim from returning to work for months or years. The law attempts to calculate the amount of money needed to compensate the injured person, not only for present medical costs and loss of income, but also for future expenses.

Punitive damages are awarded only in certain cases. Punitive damages are not meant to compensate the injured party for actual or future expenses, but to punish the offender for the act that caused the injury.

Damages for **pain and suffering** are sometimes awarded when a person has been injured. The law permits an injured person to recover not only actual and future costs, but also money to compensate for the pain and suffering he or she is forced to endure. It is possible for an injured person to collect all four types of damages in a single lawsuit.

For example, suppose Karen was seriously injured when a drunken driver ran a red light and struck her with his car. By the time the case went to court, Karen's medical costs had reached $20,000. Karen's doctors anticipated that she would require more surgery at a later date to correct scars on her face. Her future medical costs were estimated to be $30,000. The law in Karen's state permits a party to seek punitive damages when an injury occurs because of a traffic violation. In addition to compensatory and future damages, Karen's lawyer demanded $150,000 in punitive damages, because the driver had violated the state traffic code. The lawyer also sought $250,000 for the pain and suffering Karen had already endured and would again confront when she returns for surgery.

Sometimes damages are awarded to victims of consumer fraud such as odometer tampering. An odometer is the device, usually located below an automobile speedometer, that records a car's mileage. It is against both federal and state laws to tamper with a car's odometer. A buyer who has been intentionally misled as to a car's true mileage will be able to recover damages. The damages would be the difference between what the buyer paid for the car and its actual value, plus any attorney's fees that had to be paid to settle the dispute.

Suppose Monte was interested in buying a van and was shown a used vehicle that had 40,000 miles registered on its odometer. Monte bought the vehicle for $6,000. Shortly thereafter, he learned that the odometer had been altered and that the true mileage was 60,000 miles. Monte took the van to a second dealer, who advised him that, given its true mileage, the van had a market value of only $5,000. Monte is entitled to damages of $1,000 plus reimbursement for any legal fees he was forced to pay in settling the dispute.

Monte's actual damages—the difference between the actual value and the amount he paid for the car—amounted to $1,000. Some state laws provide for **treble damages** if a seller intentionally misrepresents the

If a window washer falls off a defective ladder, he might sue the ladder company for damages to compensate him for his injuries.

mileage of a used vehicle. Treble damages are three times the amount of actual damages and are meant to punish the seller for lying about the true mileage of a vehicle. Treble damages are one form of punitive damages. In states that allow treble damages, it is hoped that the possibility of a large penalty will keep used-car dealers from making false claims about mileage.

No matter how large, damage payments may not be able to correct all the emotional and physical problems a victim might suffer after an injury or fraud. But damages are an important part of our legal system and offer substantial help to those who have been victimized.

CREDIT AND COLLECTION

Using **credit** is a way for people to put off payment for goods or services until a later time. There are many different kinds of credit. Banks extend **mortgage** loans to people who want to purchase houses and consumer loans to those purchasing large items such as cars and boats. Department stores and gasoline companies issue their own credit cards, allowing their customers to charge purchases and make their payments later. National credit card companies such as American Express, Visa, and Mastercard also issue credit

Many stores accept major credit cards. Customers appreciate being able to charge their purchases instead of having to pay cash.

cards to consumers, who can use the cards to charge purchases at many stores.

Imagine that Phyllis owns and operates a small women's clothing store. Phyllis accepts both Visa and Mastercard from customers who wish to charge their purchases. This helps Phyllis because she does not have to operate her own credit system, and it also attracts more customers, who appreciate being able to use credit cards at her store.

Most national credit card companies charge an annual fee to provide the customer with a credit card. Many people are willing to pay a fee for the privilege of being able to charge purchases and delay payment. Depending upon the card, the fee can range from a few dollars to over $100 a year.

Banks and businesses also charge *interest* on their credit transactions. As discussed earlier, interest is a fee that is paid for the use of borrowed money. When people use a credit card instead of cash or take out a bank loan to pay for a house or car, they are borrowing money. Not only must they pay back the amount they borrowed (often by making monthly payments), they must also pay interest on the loan.

Banks and loan companies always charge interest on credit transactions, no matter how soon the loan is repaid. Businesses and credit card companies, however, usually do not charge interest on purchases that are paid in full within 30 days. Sometimes, interest is called a "finance charge" or a "service charge." Regardless of the term used, it is the cost the customer must pay for using credit.

Each state has laws that limit the amount of interest that can be charged on a credit transaction. Interest rates vary greatly, depending on the type of credit that is used.

Banks, for example, generally charge a lower interest rate on loans than private finance companies. National credit card companies usually charge the highest interest rates.

Open and Closed-End Accounts

Bank loans are good examples of **closed-end credit** transactions. In this type of credit arrangement, the consumer borrows a fixed amount and repays it, plus interest, over a fixed period of time. To borrow more money, the consumer must go back to the bank and take out a new loan.

In contrast, **open-end credit** transactions allow the consumer to use as much credit as is desired, as long as he or she does not exceed a predetermined "credit limit." All national credit card companies use an open-end system.

Suppose Colleen applied for her first credit card and was given an open-end "line of credit" of $2,000. This means that Colleen may charge purchases to her account as often as she likes and in any amount, provided that the total amount she owes the credit card company at any time does not exceed $2,000.

Applying for Credit

The federal Equal Credit Opportunity Act makes it illegal for a **creditor**, or lender, to refuse credit to applicants because of their race, religion, marital status, sex, country of origin, or age if they have reached the age of majority. The law also prohibits creditors from denying credit simply because an applicant receives welfare.

*C*omplete this Application for a Dayton's Account.

TYPE OF ACCOUNT - PLEASE CHECK ONE	☐ INDIVIDUAL ACCOUNT
(For explanation of account type see attached page.)	☐ JOINT ACCOUNT

Your name

FIRST	MIDDLE INITIAL	LAST	DATE OF BIRTH	SOCIAL SECURITY NUMBER

Tell us about yourself (APPLICANT)

STREET		HOW LONG	HOME PHONE NO. ( )
ADD'L STREET INFO			

CITY & STATE	CITY	STATE	ZIP CODE	PRESENT RESIDENCE ☐ Live with parents ☐ Rent Furnished ☐ Rent Unfurnished ☐ Own

PREVIOUS ADDRESS (If above is less than 5 years)	STREET	CITY	STATE	ZIP CODE	HOW LONG

EMPLOYED BY		HOW LONG

POSITION	BUSINESS PHONE ( )	ANNUAL INCOME FROM POSITION ☐ Below $16,000 ☐ $26-$36,000 ☐ $16-$26,000 ☐ Over $36,000

OTHER INCOME: ALIMONY, CHILD SUPPORT, OR SEPARATE MAINTENANCE INCOME NEED NOT BE REVEALED IF YOU DO NOT WISH IT CONSIDERED AS A BASIS FOR REPAYING THIS OBLIGATION.	SOURCE	ANNUAL AMOUNT: $

ARE YOU A FULL TIME STUDENT? ☐ NO ☐ YES If yes, School name	EDUCATION COMPLETED ☐ Trade or Business ☐ High School ☐ College ☐ Masters/Ph.D.

DRIVER'S LICENSE NO.	FOR WISCONSIN RESIDENTS ONLY ☐ Married ☐ Separated ☐ Unmarried Complete the shaded area below if you have checked married or separated.

For Joint Account Applicant

FIRST	MIDDLE INTITIAL	LAST	DATE OF BIRTH	SOCIAL SECURITY NO.

ADDRESS	BUSINESS PHONE ( )	ANNUAL INCOME FROM POSITION ☐ Below $16,000 ☐ $26-$36,000 ☐ $16-$26,000 ☐ Over $36,000

EMPLOYER'S NAME	HOW LONG	POSITION

OTHER INCOME: ALIMONY, CHILD SUPPORT, OR SEPARATE MAINTENANCE NEED NOT BE REVEALED IF YOU DO NOT WISH IT CONSIDERED AS A BASIS FOR REPAYING THIS OBLIGATION.	SOURCE	ANNUAL INCOME $

Now tell us about your present credit

HAVE YOU EVER APPLIED FOR AN ACCOUNT WITH US BEFORE? ☐ YES ☐ NO
HAVE YOU EVER HAD AN ACCOUNT WITH US BEFORE? ☐ YES ☐ NO (IF YES, ACCOUNT NO./NAME)

NAME OF BANK AND/OR CREDIT UNION:	☐ SAVINGS ACCT. #
	☐ CHECKING ACCT. #
	☐ LOAN ACCT. #

DO YOU HAVE ANY CREDIT REFERENCES? ☐ YES ☐ NO IF YES, PLEASE LIST NAMES AND ACCT. NUMBERS FOR ALL THAT APPLY. OR, IF YOU HAVE NONE OF THE FOLLOWING TYPE OF REFERENCES, PLEASE CHECK BOX. ☐	LOANS
FINANCE COMPANIES	BANK CARDS
DEPT. STORES	OIL/GAS CARDS

Your Signature Individual accounts will receive one shopping card. Joint accounts two shopping cards.

◀ I/WE HAVE READ AND I/WE AGREE TO THE TERMS AS STATED ON THE OPPOSITE PAGE OF THIS APPLICATION AND WHICH ARE HEREBY INCORPORATED BY REFERENCE AND ACKNOWLEDGE RECEIPT OF A COPY THEREOF. ▶

SIGNATURE, APPLICANT	SIGNATURE, JOINT APPLICANT

FOR OFFICE USE ONLY

ACCOUNT NUMBER	DATE APPLIED	APPROVED BY	DATE	INSERT CODE	10
	EMP. NAME	GROUP NO.		SOL. CODE	EMP. NO.	40
	☐ LIMIT INCREASE		PENDING PURCH./CREDIT LINE REQUESTED $		90

A 1989 credit application from the Dayton Hudson Department Store. Creditors look for applicants with a stable work history, a good record of paying bills and loans, and a steady income.

However, creditors may legally require an applicant to have enough income to pay the periodic bills as they become due. Creditors can turn down applicants who do not meet their standards because of a poor credit history, a prior business failure, or an unstable work history.

If a creditor refuses to give credit, the applicant must be given written notice within 30 days. In addition, the creditor must be willing to tell the applicant the reason for the denial.

Incorrect Billings

From time to time, businesses make mistakes in a bill sent to a customer. When this happens, the customer can rely upon the federal Fair Credit Billing Act to remedy the error. This law requires creditors to answer the customer's complaint promptly and to adjust the account if there has been an error.

To be protected by the Fair Credit Billing Act, the customer must put the complaint in writing and send it to the creditor. This written complaint must be sent within 60 days of receipt of the mistaken bill and should clearly explain the error.

Although it is not required by law, it is always a good idea to mention the Fair Credit Billing Act if you send a letter of complaint. This leaves no question that you intend to seek the protection of this law. You should keep a copy of your letter and you may choose to send it by registered or certified mail, requesting a return receipt. This will help you prove that the creditor actually received the complaint and will establish the date that the creditor became aware of the dispute.

A salesperson writes up a credit card purchase. With an open-end line of credit, customers may charge as often as they like, as long as they do not exceed their credit limits.

The laws of many states allow the creditor only 30 days to respond to a complaint. Federal law allows an additional 60 days for a correction to be made. Between the time the creditor receives the written complaint and the time the correction is made, the creditor may not turn the customer over to a **collection agency** or do anything else to collect the money other than send out regular billing statements. The creditor is also prohibited from suing the customer or sending a negative report to a **credit agency**. The customer, however, is obligated to pay for any amounts on the regular bills that are not in dispute.

One day Lee received a monthly bill from a department store where he regularly does business. The bill showed a charge of $25 for clothing and a second charge of $400 for furniture. Lee had charged the clothing, but not the furniture. He paid the $25, but sent the store a letter stating that, under the Federal Fair Credit Billing Act, he was advising the store of its billing error. Lee does not have to pay the $400.

Credit Reporting

When you use credit, a report may be sent by the creditor to an agency that collects credit information. Your file at the credit agency contains such information as your name and address, your occupation, your income, the number and type of loans and charge accounts you have, and your payment history. The next time you apply for credit, the creditor will examine this file to determine whether you pay your bills on time, earn enough money to afford more loan payments, and are a stable employee

Credit agencies generally keep computerized records of people who seek loans or credit cards. If a computer check reveals that an applicant has an unstable credit history or work record, he or she might be denied a loan.

who does not move from job to job every few months. If the file reflects that you are credit-worthy, your application for additional credit will be honored. If, however, your file reflects that you do not have a stable job, residence, or credit history, your application likely will be denied.

The federal Fair Credit Reporting Act entitles you to see your file at a credit reporting agency. The act also requires that the agency tell you the source of that information and the businesses that have been given that information within the recent past.

You are also entitled to contest, or deny, any information in your credit file. The reporting agency must then investigate to determine whether the information in the file is true and current. If they do not delete or correct the information after their investigation, you will be allowed to write a statement explaining your side of the story. The reporting agency must put your explanation in the file and include it with any credit report released after that time.

The Future of Economic Law

A century ago, the laws regulating economic activity in the United States were mainly concerned with large businesses and with trade between the United States and other nations. Computers that allow consumer credit histories to be transmitted from city to city with the touch of a button had not been invented. Automatic teller machines that allow consumers to obtain large amounts of cash at any hour of the day or night were beyond imagination. Laser instruments that can read prices and product information from a coded strip of paper were still the subject of science fiction.

Because our economy has changed so greatly, the laws that regulate the United States economy have changed as well. Most of the laws discussed in this book did not exist 100 years ago. As consumers in this ever-changing system, it is important that we know and understand the laws, rules, and regulations that protect us in the marketplace. It is the knowledge of these laws, rules, and regulations that will ensure that the United States economy remains the servant of the people.

GLOSSARY

age of majority—The age at which a person becomes an adult and is considered able to take charge of his or her own legal affairs

barter system—An economic system in which goods and services are exchanged for one another

capitalism—An economic system in which citizens are encouraged to invest their money in businesses with an expectation of making a profit

civil law—Law that governs disputes between individuals

closed-end credit—An arrangement in which the consumer borrows a fixed amount of money and repays it over a fixed period of time. The consumer cannot borrow additional money without making a new loan agreement.

Code of Napoleon—The laws that developed in France during the reign of the emperor Napoleon Bonaparte

collection agency—A business that contracts with creditors to pursue people who owe money

Common Law—The laws that developed in England during the Middle Ages. The Common Law is the foundation for most legal systems in the United States.

communism—An economic system in which the government maintains control over the means of producing and distributing goods and services

compensatory damages—Payments that compensate an injured party for the actual expenses connected with injury or property loss

consideration—Under contract law, consideration is anything of value.

contract—An agreement between two or more parties that can be enforced in court

credit—A means of delaying payment for goods or services until a later time

credit agency—An agency that collects and distributes credit histories of people who seek loans or credit cards

creditor—A business or person to whom money is owed

criminal law—Law that governs disputes between an individual and the government

damages—Payment made to compensate someone who has been injured or victimized

defendant—The person or organization accused of wrongdoing in a civil or criminal lawsuit

down payment—A part of the full price of an item that is paid at the time of purchase, with the remainder to be paid later

economy—The system of the production and distribution of goods and services in a country, area, or time period

future damages—Damages that are awarded to pay an injured person for costs certain to arise at a later date

implied warranty—A guarantee that is neither spoken nor written, but exists because the consumer has a right to expect that a new product will perform safely

injunction—A court order to do, or not to do, a particular thing

interest—A fee paid for the use of money

laissez-faire—A policy that government should not interfere with the economy

liable—Legally responsible for violating a criminal statute or failing to meet a civil obligation

limited warranty—A warranty that is effective for only a certain period of time or under specified conditions

mechanic's lien—A legal device that gives mechanics and other repairpeople the right to keep an item until the customer has paid in full for the repairs

minor—A person who has not reached the age of majority and is not considered capable of taking charge of legal affairs

mortgage—A loan agreement for the purchase of a piece of property

open-end credit—An arrangement in which the consumer is allowed to use as much credit as desired, as long as the amount of money borrowed does not exceed a predetermined limit

ordinance—A law passed by a city government

pain and suffering—Money awarded as compensation for the pain endured by an injured person

punitive damages—Money awarded to punish an offender for an act that caused injury or loss to another person

security deposit—Money held by a landlord or utility company as payment for damage to rental property or failure to pay a utility bill

socialism—An economic system based on the belief that a nation's wealth should be distributed equally among all citizens and that governments should try to provide for each person's basic needs

statute—A law passed by a state legislature

sue—To bring legal action

treble damages—An award of money given to an injured party that is three times the amount of the victim's actual loss. Treble damages are meant to punish the offender.

valid—Describes a contract that is legal in all respects and can be enforced in a court of law

void—Describes an illegal contract that cannot be enforced in a court of law

voidable—Describes an agreement that either can be made valid or can be cancelled by one of the parties

warranty—A guarantee from the manufacturer or seller of a product to the buyer

INDEX

acceptance (of contracts),
18-19
advance-fee schemes, 38-40
age of majority, 21-24

bait-and-switch schemes,
30-33
barter system, 6
business-opportunity schemes,
42-43

capitalism, 8
caveat emptor, 45, 46, 56
chain referral schemes, 41-42,
47
charity fraud, 41
civil law, 13-15
closed-end credit, 74
club contracts, 47-49
Code of Napoleon, 18
collection agencies, 78
commission, 42, 46 (defined)
Common Law, 16-17
communism, 8
compensatory damages, 64, 66,
67
competent parties (to contracts), 21-24
consideration (in contracts), 19
consumer fraud, 29-43;
advance-fee schemes, 38-
40; bait-and-switch, 30-33;
business-opportunity
schemes, 42-43; chain
referral schemes, 41-42;

charity fraud, 41; damages
for, 67-69; going-out-of-
business sales, 33; land
schemes, 38; packaging
fraud, 36-37; service and
repair schemes, 34-35
consumer protection, 45-55;
club contracts, 47-49; door-
to-door sales, 46-47; electronic price scanning, 52;
estimates for repairs, 50-51;
security deposits, 53-55;
unsolicited goods, 51-52
contract, defined, 16; acceptance of, 18-19; competent
parties to, 21-24; consideration in, 19; legal purpose of,
24; offers in, 18; parties to,
16; performance of prior
conditions for, 21; proper
form of, 24, 26-27; requirements for, 18-27
cooling-off periods, 46-49
credit, defined, 70; applying
for, 74-76; credit cards, 70,
73-74; credit reporting, 78-
79; incorrect billings, 76, 78;
interest on credit trans-
actions, 73-74; open- and
closed-end accounts, 74
criminal law, 14, 15

damages, defined, 64; types of
66, 67; for consumer fraud
victims, 69

door-to-door sales, 41, 42, 46-47
down payment, 38, 39, 40

economic systems, 6, 8-9
economy, defined, 8
electronic price scanning, 52
Equal Credit Opportunity Act, 74
estimates for repairs, 34-35, 50-51
executive (branch of government), 10-11
express warranties, 56-57

Fair Credit Billing Act, 76, 78
Fair Credit Reporting Act, 79
fraud, defined, 29-30
future damages, 66, 67

going-out-of-business sales, 33

implied warranties, 60-63
incorrect billings, 76, 78
injunctions, 13
interest, defined, 54; 55; on credit transactions, 73-74

judicial (branch of government), 10-11

laissez-faire policy, 8
land schemes, 38, 40
laws, 12-15
legal purpose (of contracts), 24
legislative (branch of government), 10-11
liable. *See* liability
liability, 14, 64
limited warranties, 58-60

mechanic's lien, 34, 50

odometer tampering, 67, 69
offer (of contract), 18
open-end credit, 74, 77
ordinances, 12

packaging fraud, 36-37
pain and suffering (damages for), 66, 67
performance of prior conditions (in contracts), 21
proper form (of contracts), 24, 26-27
punitive damages, 66, 67, 69

school boards, 12
security deposits, 53-55
service and repair legislation, 35, 50-51
service and repair schemes, 34-35
"short-weighting," 36-37
socialism, 8
statutes, 15

treble damages, 67, 69

U.S. economy, 8-9
U.S. government, 10, 12
U.S. legal system, 10, 12-15
unsolicited goods, 51-52
used items (sale of), 46, 61-62

valid contracts, 21-22
void contracts, 22-23
voidable contracts, 23

warranty, defined, 56; express, 56, 58; limited, 58-60; implied, 60-63

ACKNOWLEDGMENTS

Photographs and illustrations in this book are used courtesy of: Karen Sirvaitis, pp. 2, 15, 17, 36, 50, 53, 55, 59, 71, 72, 88; Lori Waselchuk, pp. 7, 19, 22, 25, 26, 31, 32, 40, 55, 57, 62, 68, 77, 80; Minnesota House of Representatives, p. 11; Minneapolis Public Schools, p. 13; Minneapolis Police Department, pp. 15, 28, 79; National Auctioneer's Association, pp. 20, 61; Bicycling Business Journal, p. 34; Tri City Advertising, Ltd., pp. 37, 44; U.S. Swim and Fitness, p. 48; Minnesota Department of Public Safety, p. 65; Dayton Hudson Department Store Company, p. 75.

Front cover photograph: Supreme Court Historical Society. Back cover photograph: Minneapolis Police Department.